A WATERY WORLD

UNDERWATER PLANTS

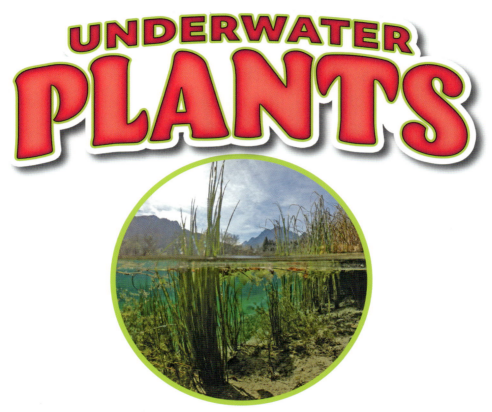

By Emma Carlson Berne

Consultant: Beth Gambro
Reading Specialist, Yorkville, Illinois

Minneapolis, Minnesota

Teaching Tips

Before Reading

- Look at the cover of the book. Discuss the picture and the title.
- Ask readers to brainstorm a list of what they already know about underwater plants. What can they expect to see in the book?
- Go on a picture walk, looking through the pictures to discuss vocabulary and make predictions about the text.

During Reading

- Read for purpose. Encourage readers to think about plants that live under water as they are reading.
- Ask readers to look for the details of the book. What are they learning about how underwater plants get the things they need?
- If readers encounter an unknown word, ask them to look at the sounds in the word. Then, ask them to look at the rest of the page. Are there any clues to help them understand?

After Reading

- Encourage readers to pick a buddy and reread the book together.
- Ask readers to name two ways plants have adapted to life in water. Find the pages that tell about these things.
- Ask readers to write or draw something they learned about underwater plants.

Credits:

Cover and title page, © Olga Ionina/iStock; 3, © AlenaPaulus/iStock; 5, © wizgeoffrey/iStock; 7, © 3sbworld/iStock; 9, © john shepherd/iStock; 11, © traveler1116/iStock; 12–13, © Damocean/iStock; 15, © naturepics_li/iStock; 16–17, © bAlllAd/iStock; 19, © Tpopova/iStock; 20–21, © Damsea/Shutterstock; 22T, © EvaKaufman/iStock; 22M, © Adisak Mitrprayoon/iStock; 22B, © Hijrawan Afif/iStock; 23TL, © 24K-Production/iStock; 23TM, © Shutter2U/iStock; 23TR, © DisobeyArt/iStock; 23BL, © mauinow1/iStock; 23BR, © kostolom/iStock.

See BearportPublishing.com for our statement on Generative AI Usage.

Library of Congress Cataloging-in-Publication Data is available at www.loc.gov or upon request from the publisher.

ISBN: 979-8-88916-991-8 (hardcover)
ISBN: 979-8-89232-460-1 (paperback)
ISBN: 979-8-89232-096-2 (ebook)

Copyright © 2025 Bearport Publishing Company. All rights reserved. No part of this publication may be reproduced in whole or in part, stored in any retrieval system, or transmitted in any form or by any means, electronic, mechanical, photocopying, recording, or otherwise, without written permission from the publisher. Bearport Publishing is a division of Chrysalis Education Group.

For more information, write to Bearport Publishing, 5357 Penn Avenue South, Minneapolis, MN 55419.

Contents

Under the Water 4

Floating Plants 22

Glossary 23

Index 24

Read More 24

Learn More Online. 24

About the Author 24

Under the Water

Tall plants **sway** under the waves.

These green leaves are growing in the blue ocean.

Water is full of plant life!

Some underwater plants grow in the salty ocean.

Others are found in **freshwater** lakes or rivers.

But all plants need many of the same things.

Plants need a gas called **carbon dioxide**.

This gas is in air and water.

Plants take it in with their leaves.

Say carbon dioxide like KAR-buhn dye-AHK-side

Another thing plants need is sunlight.

Some plants float on top of the water.

Others grow just below the waves.

They get lots of light.

There is less sunlight deep under water.

Some plants live there.

They have learned to live with less light.

All plants need clean water, too.

They take it in to help them grow.

Underwater plants have water all around.

Ocean water is very salty.

Taking in salt can hurt plants.

So, some plants **filter** out salt as they get water.

Others have a way to let it out later.

Life under water needs plants.

Plants help clean the water.

Many animals eat plants.

They use plants as hiding places, too.

Lots of plants grow under water.

They get the things they need in different ways.

Look below the waves!

What kinds of plants do you see?

Floating Plants

Some plants float on water. How do they stay up?

Giant water lilies have big leaves. The undersides of these leaves have ribs that trap air.

Duckweed traps little pockets of air within its leaves.

Water cabbages have short hairs that can trap air bubbles.

Glossary

carbon dioxide a gas that plants need to live

filter to take out unwanted things as they pass through something

freshwater having to do with water that does not have salt

sway to move slowly from side to side

Index

animals 18
float 10, 22
freshwater 6, 14
gas 8
leaves 4, 8, 22
salt 6, 16
sunlight 10, 12

Read More

Aleo, Karen. *Living Things Need Light (What Living Things Need).* North Mankato, MN: Capstone, 2020.

Mazzarella, Kerri Lee. *Freshwater Biome (Biomes on Planet Earth).* Coral Springs, FL: Seahorse Publishing, 2022.

Learn More Online

1. Go to **www.factsurfer.com** or scan the QR code below.
2. Enter "**Underwater Plants**" into the search box.
3. Click on the cover of this book to see a list of websites.

About the Author

Emma Carlson Berne lives with her family in Cincinnati, Ohio. After writing this book, she is no longer afraid of underwater plants.